You Can't See Your
BONES
WITH
BINOCULARS!

A Book About Your 206 Bones

Harriet Ziefert • pictures by **Amanda Haley**

🍎 Blue Apple Books
Maplewood, NJ

For Fred Ehrlich, M.D.,
in appreciation for his careful
review of the text and art

Text copyright © 2003, 2014 by Harriet Ziefert
Illustrations copyright © 2003 by Amanda Haley
All rights reserved
CIP data is available.

Published in the United States 2014 by
🍎 Blue Apple Books
515 Valley Street, Maplewood, NJ 07040
www.blueapplebooks.com

Printed in China
ISBN 978-1-60905-417-5
1 3 5 7 9 10 8 6 4 2

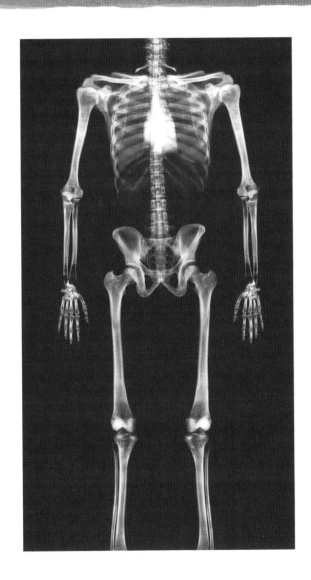

Babies have about 450 bones at birth, but by the time they
are your age, they only have 206. Why? Because many
bones, like those in the skull, grow together.

Come on a guided tour of the bones in your body...
look at the X-rays, but also make sure to stop and run
your hand along the bone or bones being described.

Put your hands around your head and push. Hard, isn't it? That's because your brain needs to be protected, and the bones in your skull do quite a good job.

If your skull were soft like a ripe cantaloupe, your brain could get mushed, and then you would have a very bad day!

Your skull, with 29 bones, has special holes for your eyes, your ears, your nose, and your mouth. If your skull were full of seeds like a watermelon, a vine could grow from your ears and nose!

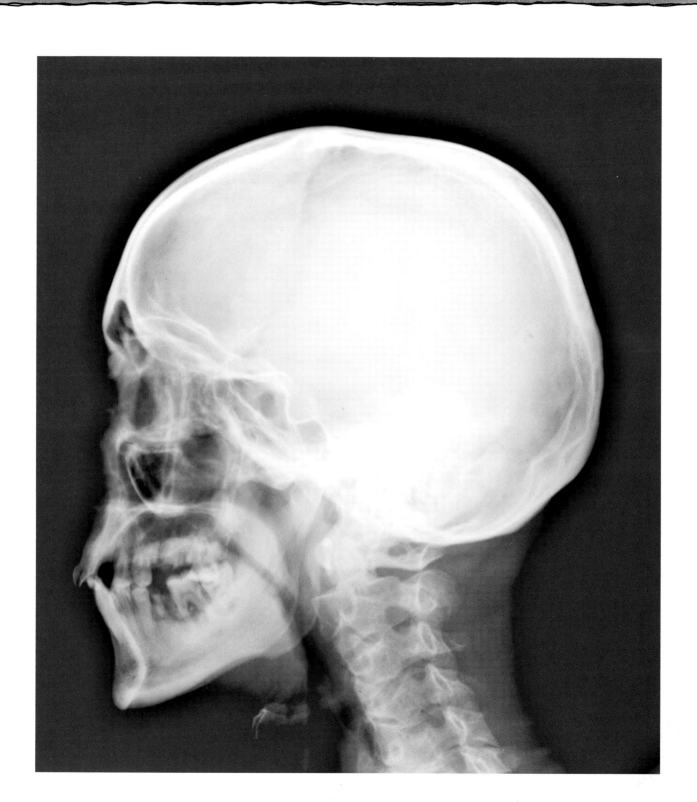

The neck bones are connected

Put your fingers on the back of your neck. The hard things you feel are your neck bones, also known as cervical vertebrae.

Each vertebra has a hole in the middle for the spinal cord to go through.

Turn your head from side to side

up
and   and
        down.

The bones move!

The topmost neck bone holds up your head. (No, not your cantaloupe, Charlie!) It is called the atlas and is named after the giant who holds the world on his shoulders in a Greek story.

Put your hand on your shoulder and move your arm around. If it feels complicated, you're right! The shoulder is very complicated.

Bones called the clavicle and the scapula come together to form a socket. The "ball" at the top of another bone called the humerus rotates so that you can move your arm in all directions.

to the back bones.

Pitchers have trouble with their rotator cuffs, which are muscles that hold the shoulder together. This trouble is because nobody told the muscles they were supposed to throw baseballs at 100 miles per hour!

The back  bones are connected

It's hard to feel your own backbone, but it's quite easy to move your fingers down someone else's. The bumps you feel are vertebrae (not walnuts, unless you have a really weird mind). It will be hard to feel all 24 of them, but it's worth a try.

Just as the skull protects your brain, the main task of the backbone is to protect your spinal cord.

to the hip bone.

Start at your neck and move your fingers down your chest. Your ribs are bones that move when you breathe. You have 12 pairs of them, and they make a cage. Is there a canary inside? No, there are two lungs and a heart in the middle.

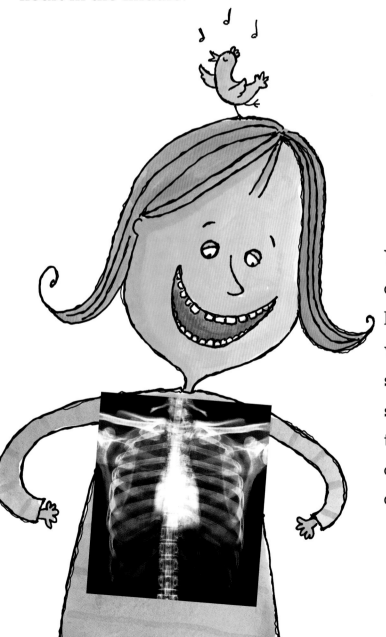

You'll soon arrive at your belly—the big, squishy place where your liver, spleen, intestines, stomach, and other terrific things hang out. None of these are bony!

The first hard thing you hit below your belly is your hip bone, or pelvis, which is made up of six bones. The rounded, hard point that pokes out on each side is the anterior superior iliac crest. If you use this word at the dinner table, everyone will be impressed, but do not try to say it with your mouth full of food!

The thigh bone is the biggest and heaviest bone you have.

It's hard to feel your thigh bone, or femur, because it's covered by big muscles, which you need for walking,

jumping,

and running away from alligators!

The knee 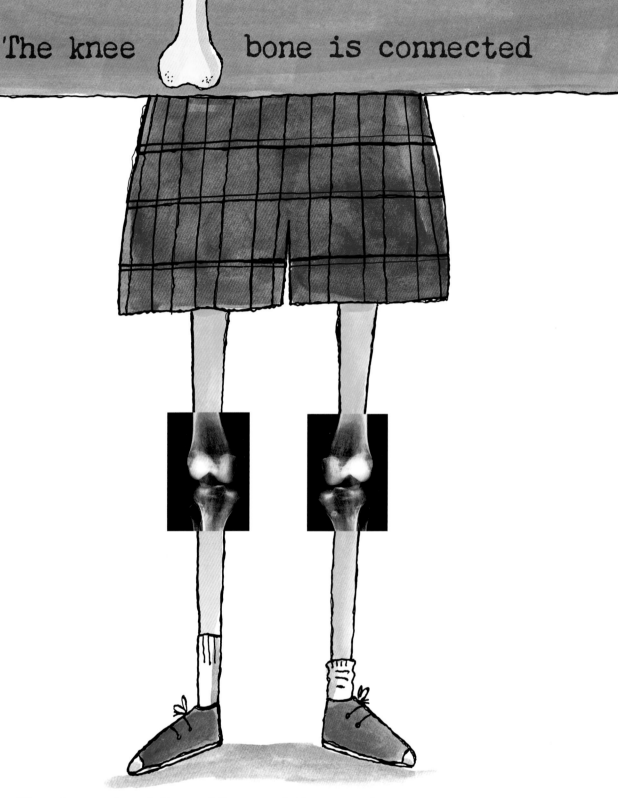 bone is connected

Kneel on a hard floor. After a while, your kneecaps, or
patellas, will probably start to hurt because there's only
skin and not much padding on them.

to the leg bones.

All of these people use different kinds of knee pads to protect their knees. If you're going to sneak out of the house on your hands and knees, be sure to wear knee pads!

football players

gardeners

hockey goalies

carpenters

There are actually two bones
in the lower leg,

the tibia   and the fibula.

You can feel the tibia at
the front of your lower leg.
It's the shin bone that hurts
a whole lot when your little
brother kicks you.

The fibula is on the little
toe side of your leg and is
harder to feel because it's
much smaller.

But give it a try anyway.

The protrusions (it never hurts to learn a new word) that people think are their ankles are really part of the leg bones. The ankle bones are hidden away where you can't really feel them.

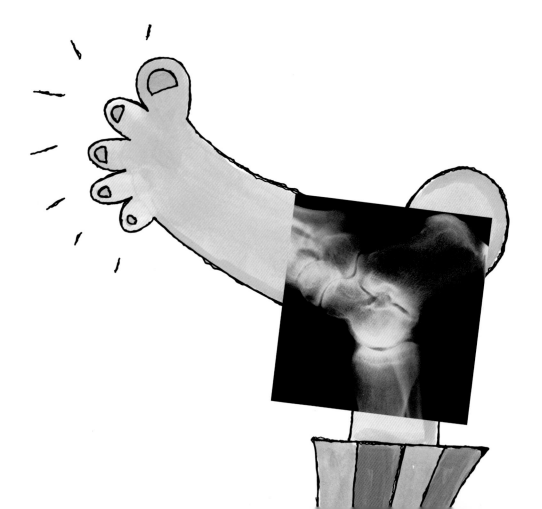

They do, however, have neat names like "navicular," and "calcaneus," and "cuneiform." But if you tell your friends you know all this, they will think you are terribly nerdy and won't talk to you for a week.

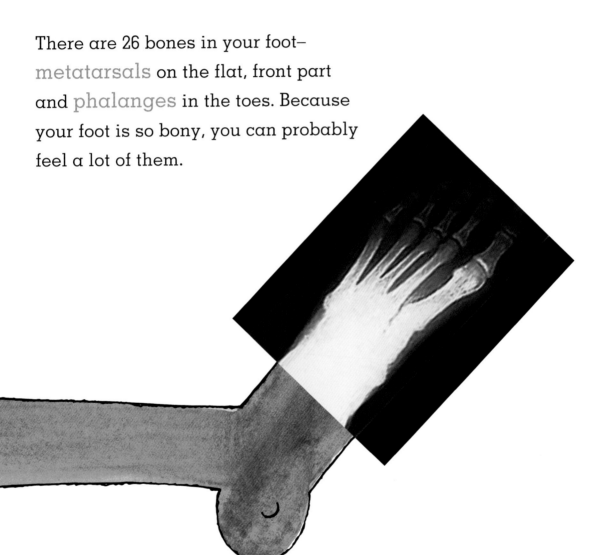

There are 26 bones in your foot—
metatarsals on the flat, front part
and phalanges in the toes. Because
your foot is so bony, you can probably
feel a lot of them.

to the toe bones.

Wiggle those toes.

Do you see your phalanges move?

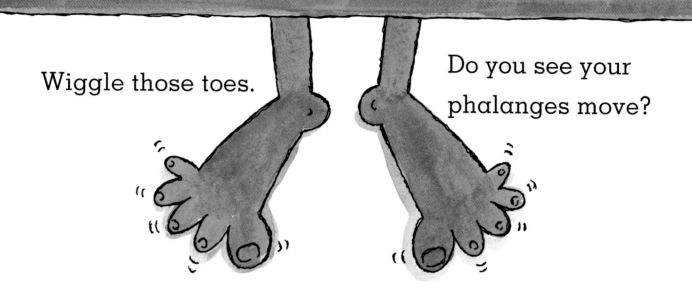

Run your hand over the top of your foot.
Do you feel the five metatarsals—one from each toe?

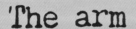

The arm is similar to the leg. There is one large bone in the upper arm, the humerus, which ends in the "funny bone." As you probably know, it's not at all funny when you bump this bone. That's because you are hitting the nerve that runs along it.

Ouch!

There are two bones in the lower arm, the radius and the ulna. Try to feel both of them. The radius is easy; the ulna is more difficult because it's the smaller of the two.

The wrist bones are connected to the hand bones, and the hand bones are connected to the finger bones!

There are 27 bones in your hand—metacarpals on the flat, front part and phalanges in the fingers. Because your hand is quite bony, you can feel a lot of them.

Bend those fingers. Do you see your phalanges move? (Make sure you bend at every joint.)

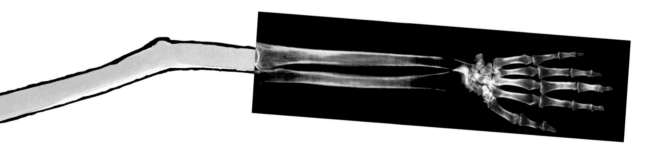

Run the fingers of your left hand over the top of your right hand. Do you feel the five metacarpals—one from each finger?

There are eight bones in the wrist, among which are the capitate, hamate, and trapezoid.

You can't see your bones with binoculars.

No...you can't see your bones with binoculars, but if you are injured, a doctor can see your bones after X-rays are taken. A bad fall or an accident can cause any of your bones to break. The area around the broken bone becomes swollen and painful.

Your bones are made of living cells, just like every other part of your body (except your hair and nails). When you break a bone, a blood clot soon forms around the two broken ends of the bone. A process begins whereby the bone cells start making new bone.

A body's repair cells will make new bone and knit together a broken bone without any help from a doctor. But unless the bone is set in exactly the same position (usually with a cast) and then kept that way for a while, the bone may not heal properly. A person may end up with one arm shorter than the other, or a crooked leg.

With the help of X-rays, the doctor can set the broken bone in exactly the right position. Later, another set of X-rays will show the doctor when the two ends of the broken bone are mended. Then the cast can be removed.

Dem Bones

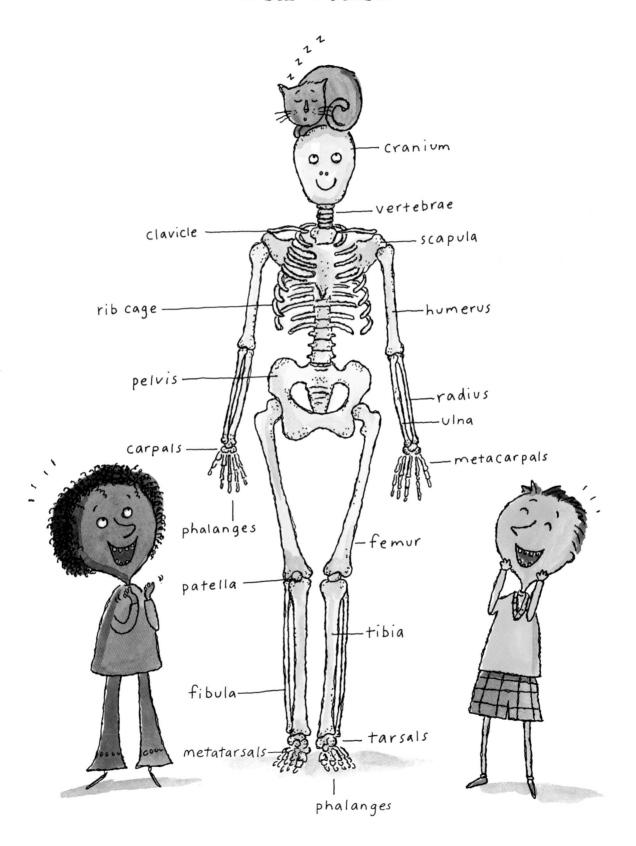

cranium

vertebrae

clavicle

scapula

rib cage

humerus

pelvis

radius

ulna

carpals

metacarpals

phalanges

femur

patella

tibia

fibula

tarsals

metatarsals

phalanges

BACK BONES AND RIBS

Human Skeleton

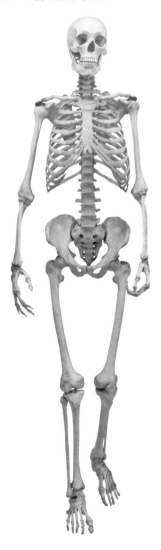

Snake Skeleton

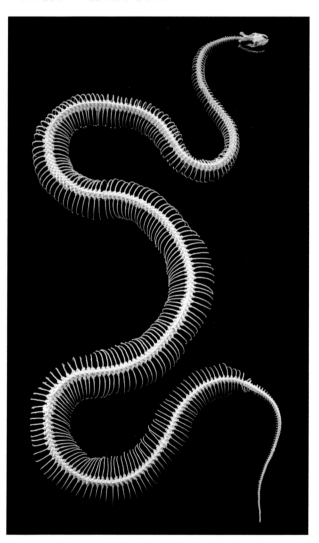

A person has 206 bones. A snake has double that number...
especially a long snake with lots of RIBS and VERTEBRAE.

What bones do you have that the snake does not?

FOOT BONES

A frog has long toes. What does a frog do with long toes?

A dog has four toes; a human has five toes.

What else is different about a dog foot and a human foot?

Frog Skeleton

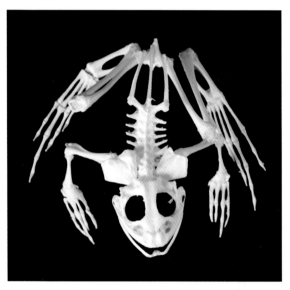

Human Foot

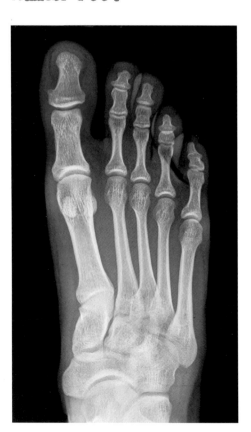

Dog Foot

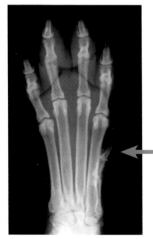

What do you think this is?

HAND BONES

A bat has wings. A fish has fins. Neither animal has a thumb . . . which makes the human hand special.

What does your thumb allow you to do that animals without thumbs can't do?

How would your life be different if you did not have thumbs?

Bat Skeleton

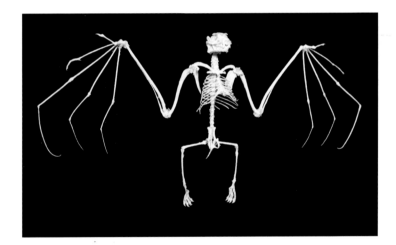

Human Hand

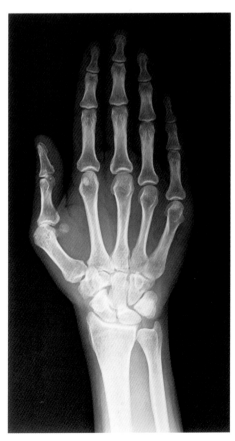

Fish Skeleton

HEAD BONES

Look at the animal skulls. Look at the human skull. A big difference is the amount of space for a brain. A human brain weighs about three pounds. The skull needs to be large enough to protect and store it.

Do you think there is a connection between the size of a skull and brain power?

Human Skull

Mouse Skull

Bird Skull

Crocodile Skull

Snake Skull

SKELETONS ON THE OUTISDE

Some animals have skeletons outside their bodies, such as those pictured below.

Can you think of others? Exoskeletons protect animals and insects from the environment and other animals.

Another name for exoskeleton is "shell."

What animals can you think of that have shells?

Can you imagine if humans had exoskeletons?

Cicada Exoskeleton

Snail Exoskeleton

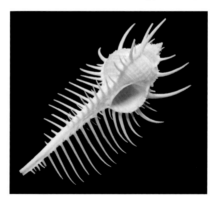

Crab Exoskeleton

WHOSE BONES?

1.

2.

3.

4.